Blessings
along the way

VICKIE PAPPAS

Phileo Blessings
Jacksonville, FL

Copyright © 2022 Vickie Pappas
All rights reserved. No part of this book may be reproduced, stored
in a retrieval system, or transmitted in any form or by any means,
electronic, mechanical, photocopying, recording, or otherwise,
without permission in writing from the publisher at, 12924 Huntley
Manor Drive, Jacksonville, FL 32224.

Book and cover design by Sagaponack Books & Design
Cover painting by Angie Hicks

Scripture is from the English Standard Version (ESV) Bible
unless otherwise noted.

ISBNs:
978-1-7377496-0-8 (softcover)
978-1-7377496-1-5 (hardcover)
978-1-7377496-2-2 (e-book)

Library of Congress Control Number: 2021924232

Summary: A Christian devotional based on Scripture,
with personal reflections to inspire and uplift.

REL036000 Religion / Inspirational
REL012020 Religion / Christian Living / Devotional
REL012120 Religion / Christian Living / Spiritual Growth
REL012070 Religion / Christian Living / Personal Growth

Phileo Blessings
Jacksonville, Florida

Printed and bound in the United States of America
First Edition

For two of my most precious blessings,
Tori and Trey,
and all who have blessed me
along the way.

Contents

FOREWORDS

As the lead pastor of The Church of Eleven22 and Vickie Pappas's pastor, I have witnessed her walk of faith over the last ten years. I originally met Vickie through a tragedy that not only impacted me then, but still affects how I live my life to this day. She is a best friend of the Wilson family, who unexpectedly and tragically lost their fifteen-year-old daughter, McKenzie. Just months before her passing, McKenzie had put her faith in Jesus through the church which I have the privilege of serving.

I know we've all been told not to judge a book by its cover; I have to confess when I met Vickie, I did just that. She's a lovely woman. Hair is always perfect, makeup's always perfect, and even in the face of this tragedy we were walking through, she was nothing but sunshine and light. I thought to myself, Who is this woman? As I've gotten to know Vickie, what I have come to realize is that the river runs very, very deep emotionally, intellectually, and theologically. The hope she has found in Jesus is unshakable. She authentically radiates a faith that is inspiring and that's rooted in an intimate and abiding relationship with the Creator.

Sometime after the Wilson family's tragedy and my meeting Vickie, I found myself on the receiving end of a weekly text she has sent out for over ten years now. Every Monday morning, I am encouraged by her devotions. They are good for the heart, they're good for the mind, and they're good for the soul. Oftentimes, they take simple concepts that we've heard before and they dive deep. Deep into the places that we may not think we want to go. She uses her own experiences, divine encounters, and Scripture to speak life to others ... myself included.

Many times in my darkest days, at just the right time, this devotional would come through and God would speak His words of encouragement and hope to me. In those moments, they were the exact words my heart needed to hear.

Her life reflects what the Bible refers to as "exhorting one another." And so, as she's compiled the devotionals that I believe come straight from the heart of God, I know you will be enriched, encouraged, challenged, and comforted if you will take the time to lean into Him as you lean into the words she has written. Trust me. You'll be blessed.

Joby Martin, Lead Pastor
The Church of Eleven22

I have told you this so that my joy may be in you, and your joy may be complete! John 15:11 (NIV)

Beautiful Vickie resonates joy. Real joy! One only knows how to be joyful in all circumstances and spread joy when one has walked through some pain and challenges. Meeting Vickie was like a breath of fresh air. She is a beautiful ray of light!

She has an intent and purpose, she has compassion and empathy, she has a mother's heart of love, and honors the Lord.

I love that Vickie has a God-given mandate: to bless, to inspire, and to encourage others. Her willingness to step out in faith, speak truth without fear, and spread her love and hospitality extravagantly benefits so many so powerfully. I am witness to having my life enriched by her weekly texts of love, given directly from our loving Father in Heaven, sent by her in a precious and personal way. God is powerfully using Vickie to enrich this wonderful tapestry we call life—with a burst of color and joy.

Be filled with joy as you absorb these anointed nuggets of love and wisdom as weekly gifts, composed into a powerful book of God deposits. The timing is crucial for all; uncertainty and change affect us more than ever before. These words point us directly to Jesus while we wait expectantly for our Savior to return.

Juliet Mayhew (Aussie soul, British heart)
Chelsea, London, UK
October 2021

The Lord bless you and keep you; the
Lord make his face shine upon you and be
gracious to you; the Lord lift his countenance
upon you and give you peace.

—Numbers 6:24-26

Blessings
along the way

Purpose

Many are the plans in the mind of a man, but it is the purpose of the LORD that will stand.
Proverbs 19:21

I believe God places people in our paths and yesterday He did just that on my flight to Dallas. I met Pastor Tim Lee, a Purple Heart Marine who lost both legs in Vietnam. He had been preaching in Amelia Island, and I am so thankful that God placed him right across the aisle from me. Tim said that God spared his life in order to serve Him and to have him spread the Good News of the Gospel. Pastor Tim Lee is the son of a Baptist preacher and, prior to going to Vietnam, had led a selfish, rebellious life, running from God. In Vietnam he stepped on a sixty-pound box mine and this changed everything. As he says, "That was the day I stopped running from God and started running for Him." Tim was actually born on the fifth of July, and though he understood Ron Kovic, an embittered paralyzed Vietnam veteran who the movie *Born on the Fourth of July* was based on, Tim chose not to be poisoned by all that had been thrown in his path. He chose a different route. He said God allowed him to experience "posttraumatic growth" in his healing journey. His story is that God took him—a liar, a thief, a person who was broken in half in Vietnam—and has used him throughout the world to proclaim His truth. Tim said: "God doesn't call the prepared, He prepares the called." I sat in awe as he smiled and handed me his latest book, written with Bob Hamer, *Born on the Fifth of July: Recreated in Vietnam*. On the inside cover he wrote: "Don't quit! Think about your purpose. What is God calling you to do?"

Purpose

Who saved us and called us to a holy calling, not because of our works but because of his own purpose and grace, which he gave us in Christ Jesus before the ages began.
2 Timothy 1:9

At my brother Billy's lake house, I met a wonderful new friend. Cindy told me she feels her calling is to help young girls who are victims and survivors of sexual exploitation and human trafficking. She shared about the organization Freedom 4/24 she is involved in, and I could feel her passion to make a difference. Cindy inspired me to think: What is God calling me to do? A calling is God's personal invitation to carry out the unique task He has for us. Are we following the call God has on our life and realizing the potential and purpose for which we were created? God uses ordinary people and moves ahead of us, preparing the way. As we desire to experience and obey God's call, we should focus on Scripture and go "ALL" out. **A** – Allow God's call to empower and change us. **L** – Leave fear and baggage of the past behind. It's a new day. Learn from our past and move ahead with confidence in God's grace, forgiveness, love, wisdom, and faithfulness. **L** – Let the Lord lead us. Our pastor continually reminds us that we can make excuses or make a difference. Will you join me in going ALL out?

Legacy

And rising very early in the morning, while it was still dark, he departed and went out to a desolate place, and there he prayed. Mark 1:35

For most of us, our mornings are filled with so many things needing our attention that we can find it difficult to spend quiet time alone with God. However, the Lord set a marvelous example for us by rising early to listen to God. I have found that when my day starts with spending time alone with God, I feel His presence throughout the day. During my childhood, my parents had a lake house, and I loved to get up early and sit by the still water. I watched in amazement as my dad skipped rocks on the surface, which left circles of ripples every time they made contact with the water. I could never do it, though I loved watching. My dad talked about the Gospel as we sat together peacefully. He reminded me of God's love and the ripple effect as it touches us and we share it with others. Ripples blend as we honor and serve Christ by serving others. This creates mini waves of love and joy. It all starts with quiet time with our Savior, an open heart, and a gentle ripple.

Legacy

One generation shall commend your works to another, and shall declare your mighty acts.
Psalm 145:4

My special friend, Angi, included me in celebrating her daughter's 13th birthday. It was an intimate group of immediate family and a few special friends. We each lit a candle for her and shared beautiful encouraging words. Afterward, as we were in a circle, her parents prayed over her. I looked at her group of friends' faces and it was beautiful; they were so encouraged too. Through this example, her parents were investing not only in their daughter, but the other young girls as well. We blew out our candles, and as I left I felt God's presence, knowing that stepping stones, not stumbling blocks, had been laid for this precious young lady, along with a legacy of faith. It was a great reminder for me to think about what I am passing down to my children and those around me.

Everything we do produces a seed and leaves something for future generations. People may not hear your words, but they are going to observe your life. We paint a picture with our lifestyles, and our children put their own frame around it. Think about what you are passing down.

Kindness

Let each of you look not only to his own interests, but also to the interests of others.
Philippians 2:4

While cleaning out my mom's fine china, I smiled as I remembered how much she loved to set a beautiful table and say, "Just like the Waldorf." That was her favorite hotel. When I was a teenager, she told me the story behind its beginnings.

In the 1880s, on a cold, rainy night, an elderly couple walked into a small hotel in Philadelphia to take shelter from the storm. The clerk, a young man, could not accommodate them since the hotel was full. Not wanting to send them out in the rain, he offered them his modest room. The next morning the gentleman told the clerk he was touched by his gesture and that one day he would build the best hotel for him to manage. Two years later, the clerk received a letter and a ticket to New York. The elderly gentleman was William Waldorf Astor, who led the clerk, Mr. Boldt, to the corner of Fifth Avenue and Thirty-Fourth Street and pointed to the new glamorous hotel ... the Waldorf Astoria.

It all started with a random act of kindness toward a stranger on a rainy night. A great reminder: You never know the ripple effects from one small act of kindness.

Kindness

Let not steadfast love and faithfulness forsake you; bind them around your neck; write them on the tablet of your heart.
Proverbs 3:3

What quality in a person makes them desirable, no matter what their age?

In a study of over one hundred thousand people from thirty-seven different cultures, kindness ranked as the most important trait. Kindness is an extension of God's love, and we show His love when our kindness is constant and consistent. Although it's an internal virtue, it expresses itself externally, in actions.

Kindness is revealed in generous thoughts that look for the good first, in sensitive words that build others up, in considerate responses we choose to make even in the face of anger or injustice, and in our intentional actions that benefit others without personal gain. We all have the capabilities, qualities, and abilities to brighten another person's day, so why not share?

Kindness matters.

Attitude

Finally, brothers, whatever is true, whatever is honorable, whatever is just, whatever is pure, whatever is lovely, whatever is commendable, if there is any excellence, if there is anything worthy of praise, think about these things.
Philippians 4:8

John Wooden, the famous former basketball coach of UCLA, said, "Things turn out best for the people who make the best of the way things turn out." Our attitudes are an outward display of what's taking place in our hearts. When our hearts focus in the right place, our attitudes will too.

One of the biggest choices we make at the start of each day is the setting of our attitude. The easiest and most cost-effective method for a makeover is adjusting our attitude. It is a choice. A positive attitude is not something that goes on around us, but rather, resides within us. We can choose to let the circumstances of life cause negative thoughts to rule our mind or we can choose to think about all we have to be thankful for. We get to choose how we respond—in other words, how we will act in regard to what happens in our life. A positive attitude helps in many ways.

The only thing we have to lose by choosing a positive attitude is a negative one.

Attitude

This is the day that the LORD has made; let us rejoice and be glad in it.
Psalm 118:24

When I went to Young Life camp as a teenager, I realized that one of my favorite songs explains the power of God's love and His joy. The song is called "Pass It On." It goes something like this: "It only takes a spark to get a fire going. And soon all those around will warm up in its glowing." That's how it is with God's love. Once you experience it, you spread His love to everyone, you want to pass it on.

This psalm reminds us that each day we have is a day created by God. It is a gift and a day we should treasure. Typically, the way we start our day greatly determines the quality of the rest of it. An optimistic view does wonders for our soul and for those around us; a negative attitude does just the opposite. Cultivating a positive mindset and thankful heart and praying throughout the day will allow us to rejoice and be glad in it.

What are you passing on?

Blessings

Bless the LORD, O my soul, and forget not all his benefits.
Psalm 103:2

astor Joby Martin is the founder and lead pastor of The Church of Eleven22 in Jacksonville, Florida. What a blessing it is to serve Jesus under his leadership. Pastor Joby continually reminds us that we deepen our relationship with Jesus as we recount His many blessings in our lives. Expressing gratitude to God redirects our attention toward Him. Our thoughts naturally drift toward our own concerns and problems. However, if we start the day by offering thanks for blessings, protection, and guidance, our perspective will shift from ourselves to our awesome God, Who loves and cares for us. Choosing to count our blessings reinforces our faith. The quickest way to dig ourselves out of an emotional ditch of discouragement and negativity is to start praising and thanking God. There is something about magnifying the Lord that puts troubles in the right perspective and reminds us that nothing is too big for Him.

Blessings

Blessed be the God and Father of our Lord Jesus Christ, who has blessed us in Christ with every spiritual blessing in the heavenly places.
Ephesians 1:3

Often, while traveling the I-95 corridor, I am motivated by the inspirational messages of local contractor Tom Trout's billboard. One in particular read: "Can't sleep? Try counting your blessings." So true, but not easy to do on our own when facing difficult circumstances. In 1897, Johnson Oatman wrote the words to a simple yet profound hymn, "Count Your Blessings." It was written for young people, to help them learn what is really worth counting and also to remember who can be counted on. His song reminds us to count our many blessings, name them one by one, and it will surprise you what the Lord has done. There is transformative power in counting our blessings and naming the good gifts of God.

Try it, trust God, and rejoice in the Lord.

Significance

Show yourself in all respects to be a model of good works, and in your teaching show integrity and dignity.
Titus 2:7

Do you celebrate the people who have had a significant influence on your life? This morning I woke up with my heart overflowing with gratitude and wrote down the people who have enriched my life and contributed to my sense of joy, well-being, and my walk with Christ. I am grateful to the people who have invested in my life and continually point me to Christ. It has been proven that we are healthier and happier when we give and receive appreciation and thanks. When we truly value the significance of the people who bless and encourage us, we expand our love of life and love of others. We are called to be people of influence—the Lord's servants who point others to the One Whose touch can change their lives. I challenge you to reflect on the people who have made a difference in your life and let them know.

Remember, a blessing isn't a blessing until it's spoken and shared.

Significance

In him you also, when you heard the word of truth, the gospel of your salvation, and believed in him, were sealed with the promised Holy Spirit, who is the guarantee of our inheritance until we acquire possession of it, to the praise of his glory.
Ephesians 1:13-14

Presidents' Day is a day to thank God for those great and godly men who have profoundly influenced the United States of America and played a significant role in shaping our country. George Washington, our first president, added the prayer, "So help me God" to his inauguration oath, and then reverently stooped and kissed the Bible. President Ronald Reagan spoke eloquently of a "shining city on a hill"; he was referring to a sermon by John Winthrop which was based on the words of Jesus Christ.

Important reminders for us on Presidents' Day are to become united people who rely on the Word of God and to deploy the power of prayer in our lives and our nation, knowing we are one nation under God.

Joy

Then he said to them, "Go your way. Eat the fat and drink sweet wine and send portions to anyone who has nothing ready, for this day is holy to our Lord. And do not be grieved, for the joy of the LORD is your strength."
Nehemiah 8:10

My dad and I took an evening ride to look at Christmas lights. We both commented on how many people had the word "joy" lit up in their yards. We had a beautiful conversation on the topic of joy. I love hearing his 87-year-old wisdom and insight. Though some people use the terms "happiness" and "joy" interchangeably, there is a vast difference in their meaning. Both cause a pleasant emotional response; however, the former relies entirely on circumstance. As soon as difficulties arise and pain intrudes, we cease to be happy. On the other hand, joy is a gift from God that enables believers to find hope and peace, even in difficult times. Amid the ups and downs of life, do we turn to God and allow His joy to sustain us? Pain is inevitable, but misery is optional. Our Heavenly Father offers a higher way of living, not without pain, yet with strength to endure.

Choose to remember the vast treasure we have in Him and His promises. "CHOOSE JOY!"

Joy

Oh give thanks to the LORD, for he is good; for his steadfast love endures forever!
1 Chronicles 16:34

When we are truly grateful for God's power at work in us and God's gift of life, we cannot contain this joy. From thankfulness comes an outpouring of gratitude that is contagious, infectious, and life giving to those around us. When thankfulness is the dominant characteristic of the interior of our life, the byproduct of gratitude is joy. Joy is the settled assurance that God is in control, the quiet confidence that ultimately everything is going to be all right, and the determined choice to praise God in all things. Joy is not dictated by our circumstances; it is fostered by the attitudes in our hearts. Nothing brightens life like the spirit of thanksgiving. Joy and peace are the beautiful results of choosing a godly, thankful, faith-filled attitude.

Patience

Better a patient person than a warrior, one with self-control than one who takes a city.
Proverbs 16:32 (New International Version)

In our fast-paced culture, we want high-speed internet, instant downloads, fast food, quick resolutions to our problems—all because we don't like waiting. We live in the "now" generation and impatience surrounds us. Impatience leads to frustration and is only a sign of our own self-centeredness. Trials and challenges that are sprinkled through life's journey actually help us learn patience. God has a purpose and a process in all things. Consider the biblical definition of patience: it can mean both long-suffering and perseverance, or not giving up and yielding under pressure. In either case it reveals itself when we are willing to wait.

Good things don't happen overnight. They must be planted, watered, weeded, and watched over. Then and only then can they be harvested. It is in the waiting that God is able to work the fruit of the Spirit in us: love, joy, peace, patience, kindness, gentleness, faithfulness, and self-control.

Patience

But if we hope for what we do not see, we wait for it with patience.
Romans 8:25

Patience is defined as the capacity to accept or tolerate delay, trouble, or suffering without getting angry or upset. Patience is the evidence of inner strength. It's interesting that some people think patience is demonstrated by someone who has an easygoing personality. But patience is not a passive trait. It is an active choice of strength under pressure. One person defined patience as the ability to let your light shine after your fuse has blown. This strength comes from obedience and trusting God. Patience is a fruit of the Spirit that increasingly develops as we're conformed to Christ's image. Choosing a calm demeanor in stressful times or while we wait can be a powerful witness to the transforming work of God in our lives.

When the "lemons" of life come, what will your response be?

Practice patience!

Adversity

Let not your hearts be troubled. Believe in God; believe also in me.
John 14:1

The storms of life are bound to hit us all at some point. The strong winds of adversity and heavy rain of affliction show no respect for a person's age or circumstances. Yet, in the midst of these trials, God offers a place of perfect peace and safety in His loving arms.

At an outdoor concert at Faith Bridge Church, singer Shawn McDonald opened his heart while singing his songs. Raised by his grandparents because his parents didn't want to be bothered with a child, Shawn said his grandfather tried his hardest to invest in him. The singer said we all go through things that hurt and are painful. In the midst of his troubles, Shawn would go to the beach and clear his head by writing songs and reading. He lit a campfire alone and, while watching the fire and feeling broken, he began to identify with the ashes and decided to let out what was in his heart. He said he didn't realize what God could do with his brokenness. He wrote the song "Rise" to capture this moment and remind us that we will rise above our circumstances.

Allow God to make beauty from ashes, and rise!

Adversity

Blessed is the man who trusts in the LORD, whose trust is the LORD. He is like a tree planted by water, that sends out its roots by the stream, and does not fear when heat comes, for its leaves remain green, and is not anxious in the year of drought, for it does not cease to bear fruit.
Jeremiah 17:7-8

How is your "root system"? When stress and adversity enter your life, do you close up? Blow up? Hold up?

Faith grows in the soil of adversity. When things are too easy, we don't have to push our roots deeper and therefore they don't develop strength. They become a weak and shallow root system. I believe when we deepen our roots of eternal character, good growth takes place. Our principles become the roots that anchor us. What we practice is what we become. Our obedience is reflective to how we live out God's commandments, no matter what situation or crisis we encounter.

Today, ask yourself: Am I rooted in God's Word? Does my behavior reflect that? Is my heart soft and full of grace? Our roots cannot flourish in a closed and hardened heart.

Encouragement

Therefore encourage one another and build one another up, just as you are doing.
1 Thessalonians 5:11

The gift of encouragement is important in our lives. The word "encourage" means to inspire with courage, spirit, or hope. Nothing can be more encouraging than God's Word shared from a loving heart. A kind, positive, encouraging word at the right time can be life changing. When we come alongside others and are truly there for each other, we can listen, comfort, console, and affirm. It's a beautiful way to live out the command to love one another.

A group of lifelong friends from our former neighborhood gathered together to celebrate our dear friend Nancy's 90th birthday. Nancy shared that my mom was the first to welcome her to the neighborhood with a homemade apple pie and me, by her side, in only a diaper and a bow. Her encouragement was an instrumental part of my upbringing. Nancy helped raise us all with her loving kindness, always pointing us to Christ. What a blessing to be able to recall the beautiful ways she touched all of our lives. As I sat beside her, holding her hand, she smiled and said, "I give all the glory to God."

Let us strive to remember the power of our words and the impact on those who hear them. Encouragement is one of the simplest yet most effective ways we can reflect Christ's love to others. Encouragement is like oxygen; it keeps hearts beating, minds clear, and hands inspired to serve.

Encouragement

And let us consider how to stir up one another to love and do good works, not neglecting to meet together, as is the habit of some, but encouraging one another, and all the more as you see the Day drawing near.
Hebrews 10:24-25

Everyone loves receiving an encouraging letter. I recently watched a great family movie, *The Letter Writer*. It highlighted the simple joy of touching hearts with a kind word and the importance of using the gifts and talents God has given us to be a blessing to others. Consider the blessing you receive when someone shares the gift of encouragement with you. It can change your focus, your outlook, and your attitude. This movie inspired me to write anonymous letters of encouragement to special young people in my life, who to this day do not know where the encouragement came from.

Those who encourage us are responding to the encouragement they themselves have received from God and others. Every one of us, young and young-at-heart alike, needs encouragement.

Choices

Look carefully then how you walk, not as unwise but as wise.
Ephesians 5:15

W
e assume making wise choices means simply learning to do the right thing every time we are faced with a decision. Our pastor told us about a book by Andy Stanley, titled *The Best Question Ever*, and it has continued to stir in my heart. The best question he says to ask is not "Is it right or wrong?" Instead, ask "What is the wise thing to do, in light of my past experience, my present circumstances, and my future hopes and dreams?" Wisdom is a skill that God gives us for operating in His world. It helps us navigate in those areas that aren't black or white. Today's culture says truth and standards of right and wrong change from decade to decade, and society is quick to stamp us as being old-fashioned. Although times do change, God's standards never do. Our choices either take us closer to God or lead us away from Him.

The choice is ours. Let's choose Godly wisdom!

Choices

It is good to grasp the one and not let go of the other. Whoever fears God will avoid all extremes. Wisdom makes one wise person more powerful than ten rulers in a city.
Ecclesiastes 7:18-19 (NIV)

*I*n Dr. Charles Stanley's message, he said when making decisions it's important to remember the word "HALT." The acronym stands for **H**ungry, **A**ngry, **L**onely, and **T**ired. We all face key moments in life when our actions can lead to lasting consequences—which is exactly why we should "HALT" when we are tempted to the point of vulnerability. The enemy knows us. He knows our struggles and tries to exploit them. Commit now not to make important decisions when we are hungry, angry, lonely, or tired. Being wise in these areas can prevent thoughts of "If only I hadn't …" later on. Instead, be honest and admit we are unprepared to make sound judgments. Then delay the decision until we can approach it with prayer, patience, and godly wisdom.

Patriotism

Blessed is the nation whose God is the LORD, the people whom he has chosen as his heritage!
Psalm 33:12

It's a famous song, but did you know it's really a prayer? I'm speaking of "God Bless America," written by Irving Berlin, in 1918, for a camp show while serving in the army in World War I. The show's producers decided not to use it. However, twenty years later Berlin offered it to Kate Smith as a patriotic song for her to sing to commemorate the anniversary of the Armistice of 11 November 1918, which ended World War I. It was an immediate sensation and has been a national favorite ever since. As beautiful fireworks are displayed to this song each year on the Fourth of July, my heart fills with gratitude. Pause to consider the lyrics, which began with this spoken introduction as a prayer to remind us of our national need for God.

> While the storm clouds gather far across the sea,
> Let us swear allegiance to a land that's free.
> Let us all be grateful for a land so fair,
> As we raise our voices in solemn prayer.
> God bless America, land that I love.
> Stand beside her and guide her
> Through the night with the light from above.
> From the mountains, to the prairies, to the
>   oceans white with foam,
> God bless America, my home sweet home.
> God bless America, my home sweet home.

Patriotism

Stand up in the presence of the aged, show respect for the elderly and revere your God. I am the LORD.
Leviticus 19:32 (NIV)

Let us remember the brave soldiers who have so unselfishly given themselves for us. Let us live lives worthy of their sacrifice. Let us never forget to show honor for their patriotism.

We took a road trip to Atlanta to listen to Dr. Charles Stanley preach on Memorial Day 2019. It was an item on my precious 86-year-old dad's bucket list. What a beautiful experience for me too. Dr. Stanley told a story about meeting a man on a Normandy beach, who was dressed in full US Army uniform. The young man said it was his father's uniform, and he comes back every year on his dad's birthday, to the spot where his dad lost his life, in order to show gratitude, honor, respect, and love. Dr. Stanley fought back tears as he recounted this story from the pulpit. What an inspiring story of reverence and honor to share in the presence of my sweet dad.

Choose to be a vessel of honor.

Honor

Greater love has no one than this, that someone lay down his life for his friends.
John 15:13

One of my life's beautiful blessings along the way was a divine encounter in 2007. I was with my parents, visiting a relative in Naples, Florida. I walked to a park close by, where a church service was being held in honor of Veterans Day. The speaker was Marine Randy Kington, author of *What a Life: How the Vietnam War Affected One Marine.*

I stood listening intently to his incredible journey, told in his southern drawl. Randy is from Tennessee. It was 1965. Randy would spend nine months in Chu Lai, guarding an airbase. During his last four months in Vietnam, he was a radio operator. He was within four feet of his platoon leader, Lt. Gary Brown, when both their lives were changed forever. Both were shot at over fifty times within seconds of each other. Forty-six men died during this battle, Operation Texas, in Quang Ngai. Randy said, "When the bullet hit me, it picked me up in the air and I began to float in slow motion. While in midair I asked God to forgive me of my sins." He came crashing down in a rice paddy. The bullet entered his neck, paralyzing Randy—then only 19—from the neck down. Life, this ex-marine said, has been a good one. In his book he included March 21, 1966. That day, the young soldier had a one-way conversation with God about survival and salvation. He reminded us that our time on earth is a blink of an eye.

One day, he said, he will walk through the gates of Heaven and into the presence of God, to spend eternity with

Him. The service concluded, and the applause continued throughout that park, in honor of this amazing marine. Randy's beautiful wife was there right beside him then, and now. She was his nurse in the VA hospital in Memphis. They have been happily married now for fifty-four years. We all became instant friends that day in the park and have continued our friendship to this day.

Randy actually chose this scripture to go with this thought on honor. He inspires me by his love and commitment to our country and to Christ.

Gray hair is a crown of glory; it is gained in a righteous life.
Proverbs 16:31

Our culture embraces the young and beautiful, but has little use for the elderly. Despite their wisdom and experience, many seniors are overlooked and forgotten. We refuse to slow down to their pace. We think we have nothing in common, and have little compassion for their physical limitations. We forget their precious value to the Lord. My friend told me how her husband took time to help their elderly neighbor in the rain. Little did they realize she would bless them with a beautiful home-cooked meal and great conversation. She inspired me to take a trip yesterday to Harbor Chase senior facility to visit my precious mom's fellow companions. My heart is still overflowing.

Will you join me to commit to cherishing the elderly? Offer the gift of a listening ear and thoughtful care. We need to stand up for older loved ones who can't help themselves. Choose to care and serve in the name of Jesus, Who loves them.

Friendship

Jonathan said to David, "Go in peace, for we have sworn friendship with each other in the name of the Lord, saying, 'The Lord is witness between you and me, and between your descendants and my descendants forever.'"
Samuel 20:42 (NIV)

A friend of mine who is a doctor met me to look at a wound on my leg that was infected. He took time on a Sunday to help me. He is a good and godly man, married to a beautiful friend of mine. I left his office with a prescription and a heart overflowing with gratefulness. Later in the day, two of my brother's best friends came over to help me. I have known them since I was two. We laughed and shared stories from our childhood and lifelong friendships. What a beautiful benefit for me, having a wonderful older brother with great friends! We have built our faithful friendships, based on God, over the last fifty-seven years.

As I reflected on the day, it was a reminder of the importance of friendships built on God's promises. Do not take these special friendships for granted, and choose to be intentional in our investment of time with them in the name of the Lord. Above all else, cultivate our friendship with Christ. His model of friendship will raise the quality of our friendships.

A Gospel-centered friend drives others to God and not to themselves. Friendships that are Gospel centered demonstrate loyalty, honesty, kindness, tenderness, compassion, and grace. These three people demonstrated that for me. I was a friend in need and they were true friends in deed. I am forever grateful.

Friendship

Iron sharpens iron, and one man sharpens another.
Proverbs 27:17

Dr. Charles Stanley preached on friendships, and I want to share his wisdom. Because God designed us to live together in relationships, friendships are an important part of His plan for our lives. Our friends are gifts from the Lord, for which we should be truly grateful. Since they are precious, we ought to do all we can to nurture these relationships and be the kind of friend God wants us to be. The most important friendship we can have is with Jesus Christ. When we walk closely with Him, we will become the companion others need and want. Great lasting friendships don't just happen; they have to be built and nurtured. Let's think about how we can actively build and nurture our friendships. If we truly love and care for our friends, we will invest our time and energy in the relationship.

In God's design, a close, committed friendship serves to build both toward Christlikeness. A good friend will walk confidently beside us, toward God's great plan. This week, think about who is sharpening you, and more importantly, who are you sharpening?

Prayer

Rejoice always, pray without ceasing, give thanks in all circumstances; for this is the will of God in Christ Jesus for you. 1 Thessalonians 5:16-18

Have you heard of the acronym P.U.S.H.? It stands for "**P**ray **U**ntil **S**omething **H**appens." Sometimes, as children of God, we go through a period of time in our lives when our level of faith isn't where it should be. Mother Teresa once said, "Prayer is not asking. Prayer is putting oneself in the hands of God, at His disposition, and listen to His voice in the depth of our hearts." God is faithful, He hears, He listens, and He is always right beside us. His timing is not always our timing. Like many of you, I am trusting Him, leaning on Him, and depending on Him in those places I cannot see.

Join me as we P.U.S.H. Pursue and trust God in all circumstances.

Prayer

For where two or three are gathered in my name, there am I among them.
Matthew 18:20

I met up with special friends to celebrate the 60th birthday of our dear friend Louise. We originally met in college, and though we live in different cities, prayer has been the anchor of our friendship. Prayer is a privilege and a lifestyle. God's power is seen when we join together in prayer for one another and for our country. As our hearts become vulnerable in prayer, we are able to have deeper, more authentic relationships. As we stand united, we should never underestimate the power of prayer, for our loving God hears our pleas. We don't know how or when He will move in response to our petitions, yet we know He longs for us to embrace His love and trust in His faithfulness.

The Lord can do mighty work through us during the time of persistent prayer and waiting.

Influence

I can do all things through him who strengthens me.
Philippians 4:13

I read the book *An Invisible Thread*. It reminded me of my relationship with JT Townsend, an incredible man I met through an incident at a football game which left him paralyzed. His wheelchair never stifled his ambition and spirit. He went on to graduate from the University of North Florida. JT always said, "You have to have a strong mind, believe in God, keep the faith, and live every day like it's your last."

According to an old Chinese proverb, there is an invisible thread that connects two people who are destined to meet and influence each other's lives. The thread bends but never breaks, and connects us for a reason. Over the next eight years we developed a heartfelt connection, though many things separated the two of us: age, culture, race, circumstance, our personalities, and from the outside we may not have seemed like typical close friends. Still, God knit us together, and JT's influence on my life was profound. Our relationship started with my family delivering a meal. Little did I know what God had in store for me. JT taught me about tenacity, perseverance, courage, faith, and, most of all—love. Especially God's love.

I encourage you, when you feel a nudge from the Holy Spirit, to act on it. The blessings I have received from JT and his family have been bright lights in my life, and it all started with delivering a simple home-cooked meal.

Influence

The wicked earns deceptive wages, but one who sows righteousness gets a sure reward.
Proverbs 11:18

There is no way to know how many people our life will influence. We don't know who is watching, listening, or learning from us. What we do and say lives on in the hearts and minds of others with definite result or consequence. Today, stop and ask yourself what you are depositing. We are called to be living examples of God's grace, mercy, and kindness. Are you a servant or do you only think about what someone can do for you? Your life will be transformed when you have a servant's spirit, giving generously to those in need, without judgment and with love. Jesus is the ultimate reflection of a selfless servant. As we reflect Him, we can patiently await our reward in Heaven.

God blesses us to be a blessing to others. That's the best way to show His love.

Gratefulness

And whatever you do, in word or deed, do everything in the name of the Lord Jesus, giving thanks to God the Father through him.
Colossians 3:17

Pastor Joby gave us a beautiful message on humility and gratefulness. He encouraged us to make a gratitude list. While at dinner with my 88-year-old dad, he shared his list, and as I wrote his words on my napkin, my heart became so full. I will always treasure his wisdom. Gratitude is a choice. One of the fundamental qualities invariably found in a grateful person is humility. A grateful person is conscious of God and others. A grateful heart will be revealed and expressed by thankful words and actions; an ungrateful heart will manifest itself in muttering and complaining. Thankful people are refreshing, life-giving springs; ungrateful people feel entitled and pull others down with their selfish and demanding ways. Gratitude is the overflow of a humble heart. I read about an African tribe that, when someone wants to make his gratitude known, he goes and sits quietly for a long period of time in front of the hut of the person for whom he is grateful. Though we may not go and sit at someone's doorstep, may we never pass up an opportunity to share our gratitude.

When we choose a lifestyle of heartfelt humble gratitude, we are mindful of the benefits received from our gracious Savior and our joy becomes full. Joy is found in humbling yourself before Jesus. The best way to achieve J.O.Y. is **J**esus, **O**thers, **Y**ou.

Gratefulness

And be renewed in the spirit of your minds.
Ephesians 4:23

A wise friend, Sharon, sent me an article on training our trains of thought. We jump aboard a train in our mind and before we realize it, we are a long way down a set of the wrong tracks and not where we hoped or intended to be.

Difficult mental and emotional patterns can teach us a lot about developing positive patterns if we approach our tendencies honestly, compassionately, and with gratefulness. At the start of each day, choose to *set your mind on things above (Colossians 3:2) and renew your mind (Romans 12:2).* The importance of renewing our mind helps us live a godly life and serve others. Gratefulness replaces unmet expectations with our greater focus on lifting up appreciation.

Trains of thought have a significant impact, no matter which ones we choose to ride. Living gratefully, as a way of life, awakens us to notice and nourish the simple things. We can hop aboard a grateful train each day. I say to that: "All aboard!"

Hospitality

Share with the Lord's people who are in need. Practice hospitality.
Romans 12:13 (NIV)

Waking up to the aftermath of a hurricane, I was drawn to one of the positive acts of kindness and hospitality that came out of the Hurricane Harvey disaster. J.J. Watt, a defensive end for Houston, had a goal to raise $200,000 for Hurricane Harvey relief efforts. He raised over $31 million and the donations kept coming. He continued his efforts and worked to fill twelve tractor-trailers with supplies for those in need. Helping others seems to be a part of his heritage. He has gone above and beyond, befriending Willa, Aaron, and Peter Berry. They were orphaned on July 2, 2011, when a head-on collision by a distracted driver killed their parents while driving home from a family vacation in Colorado. The accident severely injured Willa, who was only six years old then, and paralyzed Aaron, eight, and Peter, nine, from the waist down. Not only does J.J. supply financial support, he continues to be a big part of their daily lives. It's no surprise that his great-grandma, Sophie, wore his jersey, number 99, to church. She continues to give God the glory.

Choose to be a difference maker, no matter the circumstance.

Hospitality

Whoever receives you receives me, and whoever receives me receives him who sent me.
Matthew 10:40

Hospitality is defined as the quality or disposition of receiving and treating guests and strangers in a warm, friendly, and generous way. The very definition takes the focus off *things* and puts it back where it belongs—on people and fellowship. It is an attitude as well as an action. Making others feel welcome could be as simple as a word of encouragement, a hug, a meal, or a compassionate listening ear. In God's economy, a few seconds of focused kindness can shape a lifetime's worth of value. I want our home to be not just a place to eat and sleep; I want it to be a place where ministry happens and God touches people.

A house becomes a home by the warmth of the individual hearts of those inside.

Perseverance

But he gives more grace. Therefore it says, "God opposes the proud but gives grace to the humble." Submit yourselves therefore to God. Resist the devil, and he will flee from you. Draw near to God, and he will draw near to you. Cleanse your hands, you sinners, and purify your hearts, you double-minded. Be wretched and mourn and weep. Let your laughter be turned to mourning and your joy to gloom. Humble yourselves before the LORD, and he will exalt you.
James 4:6-10

That is an amazing promise. As we open ourselves up to the Lord, He opens up to us. If we come to Him in submission, repentance, and brokenness, He rushes in with forgiveness, love, and faithfulness. There is no room for self-sufficiency or self-protection. Only in the humility of helplessness will we discover the sufficiency of His presence. Many times, God uses situations and difficulties to get our attention. What appears to be a painful or desperate situation is often His invitation to draw near. We may feel broken, but we are never empty. If we are filled with God's spirit, we are full. It's faith in the midst of trials that gives us what we need.

For when we are weak, He is strong.

Perseverance

And we know that for those who love God all things work together for good, for those who are called according to his purpose.
Romans 8:28

Struggles and hurts are unavoidable while we're on this earth; however, we can choose how we respond to them. We can react negatively, or we can trust the Lord and see His hand at work in our lives for good. As believers, we always have God to see us through our hardships. I have a friend in the midst of a difficult trial. I have watched her faith become strengthened and she is displaying perseverance under pressure. She said she would never have been able to deal with such a big crisis a few years back, but now is allowing God to walk with her. Through His grace and power, I know she will persevere. God is in absolute control of everything and He always enables us to overcome our challenges. We must remember the world's solutions are not our solutions. Only when we rely on God's power can we experience true victory. Focusing on a negative situation only causes pain and heartache.

We must be willing to live above our circumstances by raising our eyes up and focusing on God.

Time

So teach us to number our days that we may get a heart of wisdom.
Psalm 90:12

Do we invest our time or just spend it? A day holds a lot of time: 24 hours, or 1,440 minutes, or 86,400 seconds. Yet for most of us, our daily cry is: "If I just had more time!" I have found my time spent with the Lord has a dramatic consequence in my daily life. When we set apart periods of time to pray and to meditate on His Word, we'll start to notice both subtle and dramatic changes taking place. We can begin to gain a godly perspective, not a worldly one. God desires that we invest time and energy in our relationship with Him and others. Our connection with Him makes it possible for us to live contented lives while serving a higher eternal purpose that overflows with peace, regardless of our circumstances. As followers of Christ, we have access to God's love and peace beyond understanding.

When we choose to invest our time in our walk with Christ, we can enjoy the blessings of grace.

Time

The heavens declare the glory of God, and the sky above proclaims His handiwork.
Psalm 19:1

How many days do we rush through life, outcome driven, and miss the beauty of the Lord all around us? While walking the beach late yesterday, my friend Stephanie and I ran for cover as the storm rolled in, and then we witnessed a beautiful rainbow. As we go through life and experience good and challenging times, let us be reminded of the beauty that God has given us to enjoy, and take the time to notice the wonders of His creation.

King David said Heaven declares the glory of God and the sky above proclaims His handiwork. Let us not miss the opportunities to take in the beauty of His creation. Remembering that the same God who spoke this world into creation is able to meet any need or trial. Look around and see who God is. The sky above proclaims His handiwork.

Peace

Peace I leave with you; my peace I give to you. Not as the world gives do I give to you. Let not your hearts be troubled, neither let them be afraid.
John 14:27

Often, living a peace-filled and calm life comes down to a choice: choosing to come to Him, choosing to set our mind on His Word, choosing to pray in all we face. God's Word gives strength, purpose, and grace, helping to bring an inner calm and rest to our souls. The word "calm" was originally a weather word. It comes from a Latin term meaning "hot" and was used to describe the stillness of a dry and windless day. The Bible uses the word "calm" to describe how the Lord wants to settle the weather patterns in our minds and bring us peace.

Calm can be full of energy when it's harnessed by self-control. A calm life isn't motionless or immobile; it's a choice to live life with great capacity and full of movement, while its pace is different and its motive is pure.

Peace

*You keep him in perfect peace whose mind is stayed on you,
because he trusts in you.*
Isaiah 26:3

*P*eace is God's will. Heavenly peace is a state of tranquility. It's not something that comes and goes, depending on our circumstances. It's peace of mind, heart, body, and soul. It's contentment knowing that no matter what happens, we are in the care of our Lord. Resting in God's promises gives us the hope we need to stay focused on Him and His faithfulness, instead of our circumstances. One way we can be certain we've really placed our trust in God is when we experience an indescribable peace.

In times of doubt and fear, let peace rule.

Caring

Keep your heart with all vigilance, for from it flow the springs of life.
Proverbs 4:23

To "keep" something means more than simply "to maintain ownership." It refers to maintenance, care, and support. Inside each of us is a caring heart. Finding, acknowledging, and living from it is the beginning. When we live with a caring heart, we seek opportunities to serve one another in love—with no strings attached. The caring heart seeks unity, not division. It is also free from judgment. It supports and does not ask why. It reaches out where pain exists and bears witness.

My sweet friend related how in the heat of the day, she picked up an elderly woman walking home from the grocery store. The woman told her, "I will never forget you and what you did for me today." What a beautiful example of a random act of kindness. My friend expressed it was for her a divine encounter; she feels like the one who was truly blessed.

The caring heart awaits the opportunity to serve.

Caring

Bear one another's burdens, and so fulfill the law of Christ.
Galatians 6:2

*D*id you know the first Mother's Day was celebrated in West Virginia in 1912? Mothers were to be recognized as an important part of our culture and lives. The heart of a mother is like a rare jewel. I have been blessed to witness my friend Rhonda take care of her aging mom. Rhonda moved her mother into her home months ago, and I have watched her care for her so tenderly. Her labor was borne out of love for God as she honors her so patiently. It has been a blessing and an inspiration for me to witness; her service is a modern example of the words Paul wrote to the Thessalonians, that he thanked God for *Your work produced by faith, your labor prompted by love, and your endurance inspired by hope in our Lord Jesus Christ. 1 Thessalonians 1:3 (NIV)*

Whether it is caring for a relative, helping a neighbor, or volunteering your time, be encouraged as you do the work God has called you to do. Your labor can be a powerful testimony of faith, hope, and love.

Worship

*I will give to the LORD the thanks due to his righteousness,
and I will sing praise to the name of the LORD, Most High.*
Psalm 7:17

My sweet children surprised me with a chance to see Steven Curtis Chapman in an intimate concert. As we left, I was reflecting on the beautiful things he had said during the concert. He asked, "Does it matter at all? Yes, it all matters. God has made each of us stewards of whatever responsibilities, talents, opportunities, possessions, connections, and time that we have. Every moment of every day, every decision, every task and responsibility, every action and reaction, however small, is yet another opportunity to exhibit faithfulness in all that God has entrusted to our keeping." Steven reminded us, before he sang "Do Everything," to see all of life as an act of worship, and do everything as unto Him, remembering to live as if everything we do and say matters, because it does. He closed the night with this: "As I look back on the road I've traveled, I see so many times He carried me through. And if there is one thing I've learned in this life, my Redeemer is faithful and true."

Worship

God is spirit and his worshipers must worship in the spirit of truth.
John 4:24

was listening to a sermon and the message was a beautiful reminder that worship is the life we bring to God, not just a song we sing. It's a condition of our heart, a willingness to exalt God and yield to His will. Worship is an expression of love and awe to God, Who gives us more than we deserve. We all worship something. If we wonder what we worship ... look at our calendar, our checkbook, or what we get excited about. We naturally worship whatever we place at the center of our life. God intends worship to be a lifestyle in which we constantly connect with Him. Worship is our response to who God is and what He has done.

So we ask: "How do we love God with all our heart?" We choose to glorify God in worship and in word. Where the spirit of the Lord is, there is freedom.

Forgiveness

I lift up my eyes to the mountains — where does my help come from? My help comes from the Lord, the Maker of heaven and earth.
Psalm 121:1-2 (NIV)

Walking into Emanuel AME Church in Charleston, I met two ladies who were lifelong friends. They were holding hands and dressed in their Sunday best. Delores, 88, and Mildred, 91, told me they are best friends and servants for Christ and each other.

A mass shooting occurred at Emanuel AME Church on June 17, 2015. Mildred said that although a tragedy happened at their church, they want the world to know they are a body of believers who know that only forgiveness brings peace. She quoted Psalm 121:1 and, with a smile and a wink, said, "My help also comes from Delores and her family." Her secret to a long, full life is love, faith, forgiveness, friendships, and living every day as a servant for Christ. She continued sharing that at 91 she is in the final chapter of her life, and her relationship with Christ and being others-centered are all that matter. She will keep on loving, serving, and forgiving until He calls her home. I gave her a hug and thanked her for her wisdom. It was a beautiful divine encounter and a great reminder that forgiveness brings peace.

Forgiveness

For as high as the heavens are above the earth, so great is his steadfast love toward those who fear him; as far as the east is from the west, so far does he remove our transgressions from us. Psalm 103:11-12

A sweet young friend admitted to me how she is struggling with forgiveness. Not in terms of forgiving others, but in forgiving herself. She requested a thought of the week be on this topic. The burden of sins and failures, both real and imagined, can be heavy. God is willing to forgive us if we repent. Repentance involves sorrow for past deeds and turning from them to live life differently. When we have repented of our sins, God not only forgives them, He also removes them from us. Knowing this, I believe, is the vital part for forgiving ourselves. God's mercy toward us gives us the chance to move forward. The difference between repentance and regret is that repentance leads to physical and spiritual change, while regret only leads to remorse and guilt.

Forgiveness sets us free.

Comfort

There will be a booth for shade by day from the heat, and for a refuge and a shelter from the storm and rain.
Isaiah 4:6

As we look around and find ourselves in a storm, stability and comfort are what we desire. We must realize that God is our only stability and comfort, not our circumstances. While out on a boat, we tossed down the anchor. I love the concept of an anchor. A boat anchor doesn't change the current or the waves or the winds. It simply goes to the bottom, where it is calm and quiet, and provides consistency where none seems possible from the surface.

When the wind and storms of life come crashing around us, Jesus is our anchor. If we stay fastened and connected to Him, He brings stability and peace to our souls when everything on the surface seems lost.

Comfort

For I the Lord do not change; therefore you, O children of Jacob, are not consumed.
Malachi 3:6

With all the changes in our world, there is one thing that cannot change: God. This includes His great love for us. Isn't that comforting? Every change is a challenge in some way. With change, it's comforting to know that God is in control of our lives. My friend sent me this beautiful acronym for the word "changes": **C**hrist **H**as **A** **N**ew **G**ift **E**ach **S**econd. In an ever-changing world, it is more than comforting to know we serve a God Whose love never changes. When the world is shaken, we can put our faith in Him, knowing His love for us will never change.

Vulnerability

But he said to me, "My grace is sufficient for you, for my power is made perfect in weakness." Therefore I will boast all the more gladly of my weaknesses, so that the power of Christ may rest upon me.
2 Corinthians 12:9

For when I am weak, I am strong. There is an understanding that vulnerability is one of the best things we can do to be a joyful person. Faith is the belief that God can use imperfect, broken, hurting people to do great things. God uses us in spite of our imperfection. The great physician can do a great work in us. When we are vulnerable, we are brave. When we are down to nothing, God is up to something. If we respond in faith, good things will happen. God is with us.

In 2 Corinthians, Paul talks about the thorn in his side. He pleads with God to take it away. Yet, God says, "My grace is sufficient for you." We all have thorns, and when we talk about them we can delight in knowing that when we are weak, we are strong. We all need help and it takes courage to talk about our thorns. The world teaches us to hide weaknesses, but not in the Kingdom of God. Hiding and pretending is the worst thing we can do. When we open up, we create space for the Holy Spirit to work in our lives. Living in God's strength, we move from shame to hope. Shame is silence, secrecy, and judgment. Shame is anger moved inward.

Move from silence to honesty, move from secrecy to openness, and move from judgment to grace and empathy—allowing the Holy Spirit to fill our soul.

Vulnerability

Fear not, for I am with you; be not dismayed, for I am your God; I will strengthen you, I will help you, I will uphold you with my righteous right hand.
Isaiah 41:10

Vulnerability is an endearing quality; we are naturally drawn to humble people. When we reveal our failures, feelings, frustrations, and fears, we risk rejection; even so, the benefits are worth it. Vulnerability is emotionally liberating. The most popular, most listened to TED Talk ever given was by Professor Brené Brown, titled "The Power of Vulnerability." She discovered that the most joyful, grounded, courageous, "whole-hearted" people were the ones who "embraced vulnerability." Vulnerability feels like weakness to most of us; it is not weakness, though. It takes great courage. Vulnerability is the birthplace of compassion, joy, creativity, and connection. Jesus calls us to voluntarily take on the posture of vulnerability. *Whoever wants to be my disciple must deny themselves and take up their cross and follow me. Matthew 16:24*

Cheerfulness

A cheerful heart is good medicine, but a crushed spirit dries up the bones.
Proverbs 17:22 (NIV)

Solomon assures us a cheerful heart is good medicine for the soul, the mind, and the body. To be cheerful is to be ready to greet others with a welcome, a word of encouragement, an enthusiasm for the task at hand, and a positive outlook for the future. Such people are as welcome as pain-relieving medicine. Authentic cheerfulness may show up on our faces when we smile; however, cheerfulness originates in our hearts. Once the heart knows the true joy that comes from God, that joy pervades our entire body and we can be cheerful even on the most challenging of days. I visited my friend Tracey in the hospital. In spite of her pain, she remained cheerful. When I left her I was in awe of the fountain of God's love that continued to flow from her heart. Her positive and cheerful mother, Mary, was right by her side—a beautiful reminder that a cheerful heart is the best medicine.

Cheerfulness

A glad heart makes a cheerful face, but by sorrow of heart the spirit is crushed.
Proverbs 15:13

Internal cheer involves the attitudes we choose to cultivate inside us, regardless of our circumstances. I smiled when I passed another of Tom Trout's billboards, which read: "Cheerfulness will open a door when all other keys fail." As our motives are sifted through the filter of glorying God and loving others, Christ's light will shine brightly, resulting in authentic cheerfulness.

A special friend, Kelly, gave me a plaque that reminds me daily to "Be a fountain, not a drain." The more cheerful we build our heart, the stronger it will be to help serve others. The best part is that a cheerful heart is one filled with gratitude. In a world full of negativity, remember that positive thoughts lead to a positive outlook, which leads to a positive heart.

Serving

*May these words of my mouth and the meditation of my heart
be pleasing in your sight, LORD, my Rock and my Redeemer.
Psalm 19:14 (NIV)*

A positive, optimistic attitude is not something we can just "put on," but rather, it *resides* in us. A healthy positive attitude comes from within our heart, mind, body, and spirit. It can't be bought or manufactured. However, it is contagious. Good or bad, we catch the attitudes of those we spend time with. Charles Swindoll said it best: "The single most significant decision I can make today is my choice of attitude."

Bob Williams is living a beautiful example of this by spreading kindness as he serves others. He is a retired World War II veteran, retired teacher, and high school football coach who, at 94, chooses to share his positive attitude by handing out Hershey's chocolate bars to strangers. In the past ten years he's given out nearly 6,000 bars. Williams retired from the classroom decades ago, but he's continuing to educate others in a different way, one Hershey's candy bar and smile at a time.

How can you spread kindness today by serving?

Serving

As water reflects the face, so one's life reflects the heart.
Proverbs 27:19 (NIV)

The heart reveals the real you—what you truly are, not what others think of you or what circumstances force you to be. Your heart determines why you say the things you do, why you feel the way you do, and why you act the way you do. Repeatedly the Bible says "to serve the Lord with all your heart." God wants us to serve Him passionately, not dutifully. We serve God by serving others. Pastor Joby reminded us that the best way to deepen our relationship with Jesus is to help someone else deepen theirs. God determines our greatness by how many we serve, not by how many people serve us. Thousands of books have been written on leadership, but few on servanthood. Everyone wants to lead; no one wants to be a servant. Thinking of others is the heart of Christlikeness and the best evidence of spiritual growth.

Who can we serve this week?

Doubt

May the God of hope fill you with all joy and peace as you trust in him, so that you may overflow with hope by the power of the Holy Spirit.
Romans 15:13 (NIV)

There is doubt everywhere in our world. If we aren't careful, the currents of life will cause us to drift. We don't want to drift into doubt, bitterness, anger, or resentment. So, what keeps our soul in the right place? The anchor of hope in Jesus Christ. Hope can be defined as the desire for something good and the expectation of receiving it. Christ is the only genuine source of hope. The Bible talks about hope being the anchor for our soul. Having hope doesn't mean we won't experience challenges. Rather, we choose to live out of a place of peace even when we don't get our way. Hope takes people out of darkness. Repentance turns darkness into light. Our circumstances may shift and change, but Jesus never does. He is a living hope that never disappoints.

Doubt

Let him ask in faith, with no doubting, for the one who doubts is like a wave of the sea that is driven and tossed by the wind. James 1:6

This is a beautiful reminder when we face trials, and problems are raging all around. If we aren't careful, it's easy to get mentally sidetracked. By focusing on our problems and never looking up, we will fail to experience the peace of God. The focus has to be taken off our doubts and placed on the promises of God. His words in Jeremiah 29:11 are straightforward: *"For I know the plans I have for you,"* says the Lord, *"they are plans for good and not for disaster, to give you a future and a hope."*

When I arrived at school to substitute for a teacher I admire greatly, she had written this Rex Rouis quote at the top of my lesson plan: "Hope is the raw material from which faith builds the house."

Faith

So in Christ Jesus you are all children of God through faith, for all of you who were baptized into Christ have clothed yourselves with Christ.
Galatians 3:26-27 (NIV)

My hope as a parent has been to lay a strong foundation of faith for my children. I believe, in the beginning, our children have a faith that is the same as their parents', and at some point it has to be their own personal relationship. My biggest hope is that my children will desire to go deeper in their relationship with the Lord. Faith in itself is meaningless, but faith in an all-seeing, all-knowing, all-powerful Savior means everything. Faith is the core of our lives. As I have gotten older, I have gained a greater appreciation for people who genuinely live out their faith.

Does your faith show your character and integrity to such a degree that your children and others around you see you making tough choices that reflect what is right and loving in God's eyes? Our children have a front-row seat to our life. If our faith doesn't really matter to us, then why would we believe it matters to our children?

Faith

For we walk by faith, not by sight.
2 Corinthians 5:7

While traveling, I had the opportunity to attend Andy Stanley's church in Georgia. He delivered a beautiful message on fueling our faith in a world on empty, reminding us that our faith is not only what we believe; our faith must be active. Jesus says, "Follow me," and calls us to move, live, respond, and react like Jesus. To believe is easier, but to follow takes work. When we feel drawn and nudged to step out in faith, we don't know what's going to happen on the other side. We will never know everything that hangs in the balance of our decision if we choose to step out. The one thing we know for certain that hangs in the balance is our faith. God is most honored by living, active, here-and-now faith. Andy closed his message, saying, "I'll do what I can do and trust God to do what only He can do." That's the walk that builds our faith.

Worry

Do not be anxious about anything, but in everything by prayer and supplication with thanksgiving let your requests be made known to God.
Philippians 4:6

"Just Be Held" is a beautiful song written by Mark Hall, lead singer of Casting Crowns. During his concert he told the audience that the song came out of a Bible study. He was writing it from God's perspective of singing to His child during a storm in life. He didn't realize God gave him this song a year before he would find out he had cancer, but God knew Mark was going to need it. The song connects to Philippians 4:6, which says when we're anxious about something, pray with thanksgiving. That is what Mark Hall continues to do. "Just Be Held" connects to the biblical truth found in Matthew 11:28-30: *Come to me, all who labor and are heavy laden, and I will give you rest. For my yoke is easy and my burden is light.* What comfort we can have knowing we can find rest in the arms of God, Who won't ever let go.

Prayer is a shield against worry and anxiety.

Worry

For God alone my soul waits in silence; from him comes my salvation. He alone is my rock and my salvation, my fortress; I shall not be greatly shaken.
Psalm 62:1-2

Sometimes the storms of life come without warning. In those times of trouble, Psalm 62 offers three valuable lessons. First, we must wait. The Lord acts in His own perfect time and He's never late. He will guide us to the next step. Second, we must wait in silence. When we quiet our mind, we give God an opportunity to speak His words of trust and hope to our heart. Instead of letting anxiety and worry occupy our thoughts, we must focus on God's promises from Scripture. Third, our focus is to be on the Lord, not on our troubles, ourselves, or other people. When we feel battered by the storms of life, instead of asking, "What am I going to do?"—rather, ask, "What is God doing?" Concern drives us to action, while worrying is unhealthy. We can be comforted and assured He is doing something!

Generosity

Either make the tree good and its fruit good, or make the tree bad and its fruit bad, for the tree is known by its fruit.
Matthew 12:33

Sometimes our actions are much more meaningful than our words. I witnessed this firsthand while visiting Boston. Mark Roberts and his darling labradoodle, Mocha, are "rolling" 300 miles across Massachusetts to raise money to fight hunger. Roberts set up his nonprofit, 4Hunger.org, to take action in lieu of just talking about the problem. Mark suffers from a rare neurological disorder which forces him to use an electric wheelchair. He decided to raise awareness of hunger by using the goodwill that he experiences when he rolls.

He said, "The media wasn't focused on it, so I decided that a crazy old guy with a really cute dog in a wheelchair, talking about hunger, would not only raise some money, but more importantly, raise awareness." A spokesperson for Save the Children said, "Kids can't be hungry for knowledge if they are hungry for food."

Words are easy to throw around, but it takes a righteous person to follow through with actions that back them up. Mark and Mocha were so engaging at this kickoff rally that I ended up participating in the fundraising too.

As you begin your day, ask yourself: Are my actions speaking louder than my words? Make your words count by standing by them and taking action. If everybody does something, we can make a change.

Generosity

Whoever brings blessing will be enriched, and one who waters will himself be watered.
Proverbs 11:25

Generosity is defined as the quality of being kind and generous. Generosity is an attitude of sharing whatever we have, regardless of our wealth. When we live with a generous spirit, it is amazing to watch opportunities to love come our way. Generosity in the context of godly love is much more than financial giving. When we love authentically, we have an attitude of generosity in all we do. We are alert to others' needs. Generosity involves empathy, compassion, and understanding. When generous love for others motivates our giving, generosity is not a burden but a joy. It is rare to encounter an unhappy generous person. Joy produced by generosity is the fruit of our love for the Lord. Joyful generosity grows in a soul submitted to God.

Freedom

Even as the Son of Man came not to be served but to serve, and to give his life as a ransom for many.
Matthew 20:28

On Memorial Day, we remember the brave men and women who gave their lives in service to our nation. We honor the heroes who paid the ultimate price to preserve our freedom. Fred Rogers is quoted to have said, concerning tragedies and war, "When I was a boy and I would see scary things on the news, my mother would say to me, 'Look for the helpers. You will always find people who are helping.' " Don't focus on the devastation; focus on those who are sacrificing themselves in order to help. This wouldn't be the land of the free if it were not the home of the brave.

Today and every day, join me in thanking God for all those who sacrificially loved each of us through military service.

Freedom

Now the Lord is the Spirit, and where the Spirit of the Lord is, there is freedom.
2 Corinthians 3:17

It's easy to get caught up in patriotic holiday festivities and not take the time to stop and honor our fallen soldiers with sincere gratitude. I recently read a thought-provoking comment by Ronald Reagan, who said, "Freedom is never more than one generation away from extinction. We didn't pass it on to our children in the bloodstream. It must be fought for, protected, and handed on for them to do the same." If we stop and faithfully think about the significance of freedom, it was purchased by another's sacrifice. Behind each sacrifice lies a person who gave up their life so we could enjoy ours. The love and gratitude we show those who served reminds them of the greatness of this country.

To that, I say: God bless you and God bless America.

Trust

Trust in the LORD with all your heart, and do not lean on your own understanding. In all your ways acknowledge Him, and He will make your paths straight.
Proverbs 3:5-6

God doesn't ask us to figure everything out on our own. He simply asks us to trust Him. There is great power in trusting Him. For it clears the way for our security to be based solely on Him, not on our circumstances. He is faithful to lead us and brings clarity and light through foggy times. No matter how we feel or what our current situation may be, we can be confident God's presence will go before us, paving our pathways and guiding and guarding our steps. Keep choosing trust. Let go of worry. Hold on to Him. What comfort to know the Lord is our sun and shield! The presence of shadows is not evidence of darkness, but the existence of light. A shadow is only possible in the presence of light.

Let our desire be to live only in the shadow of our Heavenly Father.

Trust

Be still, and know that I am God. I will be exalted among the nations, I will be exalted in the earth!
Psalm 46:10

We are being instructed in this verse to let go, to be quiet, and to be physically and mentally still. God used this verse to help and guide me as my precious mom left this earth and is now resting peacefully in the arms of Jesus. My mom was a loyal, loving wife, friend, and mother, and I am forever grateful for all she instilled in me. Her passion for life and her love for others will live through me. I will treasure the joyful whisper of my mom saying, "Vickie, it's a beautiful day. Listen to the birds!"

When we truly trust and experience the reality that *God is our refuge and strength, an ever-present help in times of trouble (Psalm 46:1)*, it drives fear away, shifts our focus from the world's turmoil to God's peace, and creates a quiet confidence that our Lord is in control. No matter how chaotic the world may become around us, we can find quietness and strength in our Heavenly Father's love and power.

Suffering

Beloved, do not be surprised at the fiery trial when it comes upon you to test you, as though something strange were happening to you. But rejoice insofar as you share Christ's sufferings, that you may also rejoice and be glad when his glory is revealed. Peter 4:12-13

My friend Jeanette lost everything she owned in a house fire. She and her two children barely escaped. Sadly, her beloved dog and cat didn't make it out. I asked her permission to write about her ordeal, and she was eager to share how she has witnessed God's hand and love like never before. Instead of focusing on the loss, she is focusing on the hope that can be found in the most disastrous of circumstances—like the kindness of others who have come to lift them back to their feet. She said the real reason people have been so compelled to reach out and extend their resources is because God is speaking to their hearts. Accepting everyone's love, support, and gifts allows God's love to shine through them. Jeanette said, "No fire can take away our ability to love, dream, and hope. My children and I are the fortunate ones, as we have front row seats to the work God is doing through others. I will be forever grateful to have witnessed this most incredible event in our lives." After dropping off a basket of necessities for her family, I was inspired by her strong faith, even in the midst of a catastrophic house fire. She left me with this: "Every tragedy holds an opportunity for us to learn and grow, and Christ supplies beauty for ashes."

Suffering

Draw near to God, and he will draw near to you. Cleanse your hands, you sinners, and purify your hearts, you double-minded. James 4:8

That is an amazing promise. As we open ourselves up to the Lord, He opens up to us. If we come to Him in submission, repentance, and brokenness, He rushes in with forgiveness, love, and faithfulness. There is no room for self-sufficiency or self-protection. Only in the humility of helplessness will we discover the sufficiency of His presence. Many times, God uses situations and difficulties to get our attention. Pain, pruning, sorrow, and tragedy strengthen our faith and increase our resilience. What appears to be a painful or desperate situation is often His invitation to draw near. We may feel broken, yet we are never empty. If we are filled with God's spirit, we are full. It's faith in the midst of trials that gives us what we need.

Wisdom

Instruct the wise and they will be wiser still; teach the righteous and they will add to their learning. The fear of the Lord is the beginning of wisdom, and knowledge of the Holy One is understanding.
Proverbs 9:9-10 (NIV)

What a treat to enjoy a trip with special lifelong friends to Clearlake, Indiana. Life has a way of slowing down and simplifying when you're by the water. As we sat outside for an annual outdoor church service, we could feel the heavenly warmth on our faces and revel in the beauty that surrounded us. Rev. Jeffrey Corder shared a message titled "A Word to the Wise." He began with this story: One day, a group of high school students returned from a mission trip they had taken with their church. As one of the boys was hauling his luggage over, the pastor put an arm on his shoulder and said, "Son, today I'm going to teach you how to steal, drink, lie, and swear." "What!" exclaimed the shocked young man. The pastor said, "I'm going to teach you how to steal time out of every day to read a chapter in the book of Proverbs, to drink in the wisdom of Solomon, to lie down in your bed and meditate on the truth you discovered there, and to swear by the grace of God to put it into action."

Actually, that sounds like pretty wise advice, doesn't it? Singer-songwriter Cheré Pepper ended the service singing an original song, "You Did It All," with her hair blowing in the wind, in front of a wooden cross. What a beautiful way to seek the one who refreshes our souls and renews our hearts.

Wisdom

Do not forsake wisdom, and she will protect you; love her, and she will watch over you. The beginning of wisdom is this: Get wisdom. Though it cost all you have, get understanding.
Proverbs 4:6-7 (NIV)

The Lord speaks to us through the Bible. It's the best place to find wisdom. If we are inattentive to God's Word, then we have turned away from our major source of hearing from God. When we open His Word, we hear how much He loves us. From Scripture, we will receive definite direction for our lives. God wants to provide us with His wisdom so we will make the right decisions. God also talks to us to give us the reassuring and comforting words we so desperately need. He sees our trials, our failures, and our sorrows; He wants to speak words of loving truth to us.

The question is, "Are we listening?"

Words

Gracious words are like a honeycomb, sweetness to the soul and health to the body.
Proverbs 16:24

Scripture reminds us that our words are powerful. We can know our words are refreshing and seasoned with grace when our tone and manner reflect kindness. By sowing good, pleasant seeds in others, we reap the harvest God has prepared for us. In God's garden, plant three rows of squash: squash gossip, squash criticism, and squash indifference. Plant seven rows of peas: prayer, promptness, perseverance, politeness, preparedness, purity, and patience. And plant seven rows of lettuce. Let us be faithful. Let us be unselfish. Let us be loyal. Let us be truthful. Let us search Scriptures. Let us not be weary in doing well. Let us love one another.

Look for good and kind things to say about others, remembering to go to God's garden and plant His love everywhere we go.

Words

The tongue has the power of life and death, and those who love it will eat its fruit.
Proverbs 18:21 (NIV)

Pastor Joby reminded us about the power of our words as they reveal our hearts. Words are powerful. We have the power to either encourage or destroy others with our speech. Kind, positive, encouraging words can truly be life-changing. There is hardly anything in the world that costs less, yet is worth more than a kind word. Kind words are a blessing upon both the speaker and the listener. You may never know what profound effects your kind words carry. You utter them and go on your way, leaving them to work their magic.

Let us all remember the power of our words and their influence on those who hear them.

Love

This is my commandment, that you love one another as I have loved you.
John 15:12

Our church is doing a great series on love. Love that sticks. I have been having fun with the sticky notes they gave us to leave behind for others as encouragement—a great reminder that love requires action. It's not a thing we try to get for ourselves; instead, it is an action we express to others through thanksgiving, caring, serving, and sharing. We love because God first loved us. To walk in love often paints a picture of self-sacrifice. For example, actions like ignoring insults, not taking offense, and still doing the right thing to those who have wronged us are ways we honor Jesus—by following His example. When we choose to follow His lead, we can live in an atmosphere of joy. It takes resentment and bitterness out of passion and instead injects it with grace and mercy, which causes love to prosper.

Let's make an effort to put action back into our understanding of love, and love others by our actions. Concentrate on what God sees and feels for us and for each other instead of what we feel. Let's choose love!

Love

Love bears all things, believes all things, hopes all things, endures all things.
1 Corinthians 13:7

I am big on love. I have read all the Scriptures I could find on the topic and now I am even more convinced that love is the real purpose in living. Without love and all its magnificent qualities, life is meaningless and boring. We need to overthrow the dominance of selfish, self-centered living that society supports. Nothing will change in our world unless we are willing to change. I think if we all knew how to receive and give love, our world would be a different place. Love must be seen and felt. God is love. Love is and has always been His idea. He came to love us, to teach us how to love Him, and to teach us how to love ourselves and others. When we do this, life is beautiful. Love is the answer to selfishness because love gives while selfishness takes. Life should not be all about what others can do for us; it must be about what we can do for others. We are called to be God's ambassadors, and our goals should be to love people; be a giver, not a taker; and try to add to the lives of those around us.

What are you doing to make someone else's life better?

Gentleness

Be completely humble and gentle; be patient, bearing with one another in love.
Ephesians 4:2 (NIV)

God cannot fill a closed fist with good things. The moment our hands are clenched tight, fingers all pointing toward self and our rights and demands, joy is snuffed out. When we close our hand tightly, trying to protect, control, and shield, we will find that palms closed into protective fists only fill with darkness. Joy is a flame that glimmers only in the palm of the open hand. In an open and humble palm in submissiveness to His will, He will fill our emptiness with Himself. My daughter, Tori, and I visited her elderly neighbor, whose hands were closed tightly. As we gently joined hands to pray with her, I could feel the Holy Spirit move as she opened her frail and tightly clenched hands. I choose to humbly open my hands to release my will and to receive His.

This is a good reminder of the power of a gentle touch from a loving heart.

Gentleness

Let your gentleness be evident to all. The Lord is near.
Philippians 4:5 (NIV)

Gentleness becomes apparent to other people through our actions. Gentleness is a mildness of temperament. The mildness comes from an internal calm and care for others. It's a strong hand with a soft touch. Did you know that sea otters gently hold hands while they sleep, to keep each other from drifting away? Gentleness is a tender, compassionate approach toward others. We can bear this fruit through the Holy Spirit living within us. Letting it show brings glory to God and fulfills His will. Gentleness is contagious and will always find ways to spread.

Obedience

If you are willing and obedient, you shall eat the good of the land.
Isaiah 1:19

Obedience is the beginning of all spiritual blessings. When we obey God—regardless of what He asks us to do—blessings come. Blessings reinforce behavior. What we give to others as a result of our obedience to God is never lost. It leaves our hands temporarily, but it never leaves our life. We give it, God uses it to bless someone else, and we are blessed in return.

As we understand this great principle, may God be the needle and we be the thread, following Him wherever He leads.

Obedience

Whatever you do, work heartily, as for the Lord and not for men.
Colossians 3:23

The theme of the Christian life is serving Christ by serving others. Jesus came to earth to serve others: by His love, His teaching, His healing, and, ultimately, His death. The Word of God describes believers as ambassadors, soldiers, and saints. The highest honor we can receive is to be called servants of the Most High, God. A good servant shares both Jesus Christ's attitude of humility and His motivation to reach people with the love of God.

How do we know if we have the heart of a servant?

Endurance

Not only that, but we rejoice in our sufferings, knowing that suffering produces endurance, and endurance produces character, and character produces hope.
Romans 5:3-4

There are so many virtues, as Christians, we aspire to have. Who doesn't want to be known as loving, compassionate, joyful, or gracious? But I don't think there are many of us who long to endure. The word brings up images of hardship because endurance is often how we cope with things we don't like, such as criticism, conflict, pain, and illness. The way we handle adversities makes a huge difference in our life. If we shrink back, choose to be bitter and negative, we are allowing the difficulties of life to bury us. Alternately, when we choose to keep pressing forward, trusting and praising God even in the hard times, we are allowing God's character to develop inside us.

My friend, Billie Jo, said that the only difference between a piece of black coal and a priceless diamond is the amount of pressure it has endured. When we stand strong in the midst of trials and difficulties in life, when we allow God to shape our character, it's like going from a piece of coal to a diamond. When our goal is to grow in Christ and become who He wants us to be, we'll find ourselves willing to endure adversities because the outcome will be worth it.

Endurance

But Jesus looked at them and said, "With man this is impossible, but with God all things are possible."
Matthew 19:26

A divine encounter one Father's Day led us to someone special. Tyrone was broken, homeless, and just released from prison when my dad, my son Trey, and I crossed Tyrone's path at the 7-Eleven. He had a wooden cross around his neck, yet was clearly despondent. What began as a casual conversation evolved into a beautiful faith-based friendship.

Tyrone now works full-time and was recently promoted to supervisor at his job in Folkston, Georgia. My dad and I had the pleasure of enjoying dinner with Tyrone and his family. Tyrone shared about his daily Bible reading and desire to influence others to Christ. Tyrone acknowledged that without endurance to keep going, trusting God, and the divine encounter with my dad—whom he refers to as "Pops"—he would never be the man he is today.

Watching Tyrone turn his life around while giving God the glory is both wonderful and inspiring.

Grace

The grace of our Lord Jesus Christ be with you all. Amen.
Revelation 22:21

While standing outside the Emanuel AME Church in Charleston, I met a lovely, soft-spoken lady and relative of one of the victims of the 2015 shooting. She goes to church every Wednesday and Sunday night to pray and honor her grandmother. She told me that when we suffer injustice, our human heart craves revenge, vindication, and retaliation. These are also desires Christ died to free us from. We are commanded to respond to injustice with forgiveness. Though still in deep mourning, she said that forgiveness is an extension of love because this is God's disposition toward us every day. God is love and He calls His people to love. She said she is free of hate and instead empowered by love because that is what her grandmother stood for. We hugged, and I walked away so inspired by her deep faith and pure heart. I used to view Charleston as the neat city where my son goes to school; now I see Charleston as a city full of grace, love, and unity. As I passed the flowers and wreaths that surrounded the church, there stood a large sign: DON'T DENY, UNIFY. That is exactly what I had witnessed.

Grace

Let us then with confidence draw near to the throne of grace, that we may receive mercy and find grace to help in time of need.
Hebrews 4:16

I bought a lemonade from a precious little girl named Grace. I told her I loved her name, and, with a smile, she said, "My mom says everyone needs grace." I thought about that all day. What is grace? Grace is the unmerited favor of God. The best way to describe it is by using the very letters that make up the word "G-R-A-C-E": **G**od's **R**iches **A**t **C**hrist's **E**xpense. Our faith teaches us that grace can only come from God. Grace is not only God's disposition to do good for us when we don't deserve it, an undeserved favor, it is also a power from God that acts in our lives and makes good things happen in us and for us. There is power in grace and mercy together; they will set us free from sin, guilt, and shame.

Praise God for mercy and grace ... something I need every day.

Hope

We have this hope as an anchor for the soul, firm and secure. A hope that enters into the inner place behind the curtain. Hebrews 6:19 (NIV)

To center our lives around God is to build our foundation on the unshakable center of all eternity. While away in the mountains of North Georgia, I was reminded of that. Surrounded by close friends and the beauty of God's creation, I had time to rediscover the rich lessons found in nature. Seeking God while outdoors and marveling at the beauty of His creation certainly soothes and inspires me. The rays of sunshine bring hope to my heart and warmth to my soul. Spiritual growth happens best when we recognize that God is with us always.

Our trip ended with a visit to Milo's Homestyle Restaurant. I asked the owner how they got their name and, with a big smile, she replied, "Milo's stands for **M**ighty, **I**ncorruptible, **L**oving, **O**mnipotent **S**avior." I gave her a hug and left inspired to continue building my life around encounters with Jesus. In doing so, I place the anchor of my hope in the King of Kings and Lord of Lords.

Over many years of friendship, my friends' home has been a beautiful respite centered on faith, hope, and hospitality. Their faith is an inspiration to many. Thank you to the Terrys for a fabulous weekend!

Hope

For we are his workmanship, created in Christ Jesus for good works, which God prepared beforehand, that we should walk in them.
Ephesians 2:10

How do we sprinkle drops of hope onto the desert of a person's soul? It may begin with a smile, a kind word, or an act of kindness. The realization that each person is uniquely formed in the image of God is an incredible motivation to dispense hope in a desperate world.

I read about a young girl named Mackenzie. She suffers from Sotos syndrome and has trouble making friends at school. Sadly, no one responded "yes" to Mackenzie's tenth-birthday invitation. Her mom decided to post her party on Facebook and invite girls around her age to come. That's when the unexpected happened—more than four hundred guests came to celebrate her. Sam's Club donated the food; Elsa, a performer from *Frozen*, donated her time; and the mayor declared it "Mackenzie Day." Through tears, the girl's mom said, "We all want the same thing, to be loved and accepted." Mackenzie had tears of joy, standing by and wearing a shirt that read: "Be Kind and Courageous."

Is there someone you are aware of who is being left out or neglected?

Humility

And let us not grow weary of doing good, for in due season we will reap, if we do not give up.
Galatians 6:9

Humility comes when we decide life is not about what we want, but ultimately about what God wants to do in and through us. The word "goodness" refers to excellence in character shown through means of works of humble kindness. When we act out of true goodness of our heart and reflect the fruit of the Spirit, we are obedient to God's commands and seek the benefit of others. Our actions come from selflessness, placing the needs of others above our own. True humility doesn't make you think less of yourself; it makes you think of yourself less. It is not about doing elaborate things to gain recognition. Oftentimes, the small acts of goodness we do throughout our day mean the most. It's in these acts of goodness that we reflect God's character and possess the fruit of the Spirit.

Humility

Blessed are the meek, for they shall inherit the earth.
Matthew 5:5

As the Holy Spirit continues to increase our faithfulness, we realize that forcefulness is not a virtue. Meekness is. Some people associate meekness with weakness or backing down. Actually, the opposite is true. Meekness provides the strength we need to stand in the position God has placed us. Meekness is the power to absorb adversity and criticism without lashing back. Humility allows us to confidently pursue God's purpose, knowing God will open the doors of opportunity we need in order to make it happen. Without Him, we can do nothing; with Him, we can do ALL things.

Compassion

Be kind and compassionate to one another, forgiving each other, just as in Christ God forgave you.
Ephesians 4:32 (NIV)

This is such a common Bible verse, yet we seem to live in a world where rudeness and selfishness is common. Compassion is important to me. I have seen how tenderness often does the most amazing things. A friend came to repair my floor and he brought along his cousin from Colombia. Though I was busy, I could tell Duvan wanted me to talk to his friend. It was his first time in America, and he said he didn't want to go home. He loves God and felt so blessed to be here. He told us how he loves his family and loves to dance. He spoke no English so our conversation came through translation. He smiled. I felt God nudge me to ask what size shoes he wears. It just so happened that my son, Trey, had outgrown a beautiful pair of dress shoes that were the exact size of my new friend's feet. He slipped them on, smiling and dancing in my bathroom. Though he left with new shoes, I received the bigger blessing. It truly is so much better to give than to receive!

This is a great reminder of the small differences we can make if we choose to take the time to be tenderhearted. We may not be able to help everyone, yet we can positively affect some people simply by our choices, attitudes, and actions.

Compassion

Finally, all of you, have unity of mind, sympathy, brotherly love, a tender heart, and a humble mind.
1 Peter 3:8

I read where every 34 seconds, someone in the United States suffers from a heart attack. I almost lost my dear friend Joye to one. Let's make sure we not only evaluate our heart's physical health, but also our heart's spiritual health. Inside each of us is a caring heart. Finding, acknowledging, and living from it is the beginning. When we live with a caring heart, we are open, dear, compassionate, and united. We seek opportunities to serve one another in love. The caring heart supports and doesn't ask why. It reaches out where pain exists and bears witness. The caring heart remains vulnerable even at the risk of being broken. It seeks unity, not division. It is free from judgment and full of God's mercy and grace.

I did a heart check, and I hope you will too. Since our heart is so important to what we think, say, and do, we need to do open-heart surgery at the hand of our Lord.

Protection

My God, my rock, in whom I take refuge, my shield, and the horn of my salvation, my stronghold and my refuge, my savior; you save me from violence.
2 Samuel 22:3

God faithfully watches over us. He is always with us—strengthening, refreshing, encouraging, and protecting. When troubles come and even appear dangerous, what comfort we have in the promises of God. Before McKenzie Wilson went to be with the Lord in 2010, she purchased a turquoise cross to hang on the rear-view mirror of the car she would soon be able to drive. Not only to make her faith public, but to protect her under God's mighty hand. Although she went to be with Jesus before she could drive, a few close friends got together and had the cross replicated as a reminder of this faithful servant and of our mighty Lord. Thousands of crosses can be seen all over Jacksonville now, years later, as a tribute to McKenzie's faith. A friend asked to buy ten of the McKenzie crosses which I keep stored in my garage. She stood in my driveway and shared that her close friend's daughter was involved in an accident where her car was totaled, but she crawled out with only an injured foot. The one thing remaining from the wreckage was her McKenzie cross hanging from the rear-view mirror. Her mom wanted these ten crosses to give to each of her friends as a reminder that God is always watching out for them.

My cross hangs in my car as a reminder of McKenzie's bold faith, her love, and legacy.

Protection

He who dwells in the shelter of the most high will rest in the shadow of the almighty.
Psalm 91:1

*P*rayerfully meditating on Psalm 91 always brings a divine light and peace to my soul. What comfort we have in God's protection and loyalty. In 1998, I met Judi Zitiello and have been blessed by her friendship over the years. Her story is miraculous. In 2013, she was diagnosed with pancreatic cancer. This came as a complete shock, as she has always been active, healthy, and vibrant. After a nine-and-a-half-hour pancreaticoduodenectomy surgery, she said it was her faith, this psalm, and the power of prayer that got her through. What better place, she said, than to rest under Jesus's feathers; it brought her comfort and peace, no matter the outcome. When she woke up after the surgery, she only saw white light and felt like she was wrapped in a cocoon. She asked if she was in Heaven. Her sweet husband, Tom, replied, "No, you are here with me!" Judi's answer … "Praise God," as she extended her hands up to the Lord.

God continues to use her daily to connect dots, people, resources, research, and projects. Her faith is her foundation. God led her through peaks and valleys, protecting and refining her along the way. She said it's not her story, it's HIS story, a testament to faith, grace, trust, and belief as she lives life daily to the fullest, under His feathers of protection.

Contentment

But godliness with contentment is great gain, for we brought nothing into the world, and we cannot take anything out of the world.
1 Timothy 6:6-7

A blessing along the way was meeting Pam and Ricky Ruby in the Charlotte airport in 2020. Ricky was headed to Mayo Clinic for an emergency checkup for his kidney transplant that appeared to be failing. He was a kind, gentle man who overheard me on the phone with my dad about his kidney checkup at Mayo earlier that day. Ricky spoke softly and offered encouragement as he told of his journey. Little did I know that he and his wife Pam would end up staying with me because their lodging at Mayo was unexpectedly given away. Over the next few days we sat at my kitchen table as he shared his testimony and secret.

While on oxygen support, he said, "Fear of dying or anything else will rob you of the joy of living." His secret was contentment. True contentment is a choice, an inner sense of rest and peace that comes from God. My dad and I sat in awe as he said, "Don't look back. Living with the should-haves, could-haves, or would-haves will only lead to wallowing in regrets. Instead, listen to God's voice and promises. By His power and strength, true contentment is available."

It may take a shift in perspective and a change of heart, but true contentment will give you the opportunity to live every day to the fullest. What a witness Ricky Ruby was to me and so many lives I know that he touched on earth. He is now resting contently in the arms of Jesus.

Contentment

For the sake of Christ, then, I am content with weaknesses, insults, hardships, persecutions, and calamities. For when I am weak, then I am strong.
2 Corinthians 12:10

There is a power available to every heart that believes. It's available to the poor and the wealthy, the strong and the weak, the unknown and the famous, to those with much and to those with little. What is this power, you ask? It is the power of contentment. What does contentment bring to your life? It brings the power of a quiet heart. It's an inner sense of sufficiency that comes from peace in God. It takes you to still waters, not crashing waves; to satisfaction, not dissatisfaction; and it helps edify, rectify, and sanctify our soul. It's not based on our bank account, report card, paycheck, or assets because all these things can change in a moment. Contentment is based on God's truth. The Bible tells us: *I can do all things through Christ who strengthens me. (Philippians 4:13)* God is my provider, and I trust in Him alone.

Always remember God is our best source of encouragement and contentment.

Actions

Now there are varieties of gifts, but the same spirit; and there are varieties of service, but the same Lord; and there are varieties of activities, but it is the same God who empowers them all in everyone.
1 Corinthians 12:4-6

*I*t warmed my heart to hear about an 18-year-old food server, regarding her random act toward an elderly customer at Waffle House. She not only brought him his breakfast, but when he was having trouble, without hesitation she cut up his ham.

Another customer who witnessed this compassion said that although it may have seemed small, to this elderly man who was alone and on oxygen, her gesture was huge. The customer posted: "I am thankful to have seen this act of kindness and caring at the start of my day, while everything in this world seems so negative." The young woman said she didn't expect any recognition. It simply came from her heart.

As a thank-you gesture in recognition for her thoughtfulness, Texas Southern University presented her with a $16,000 scholarship. She accepted graciously and can still be found working proudly at Waffle House on the morning shift.

Each day offers us opportunities for random acts of kindness.

Actions

By this all people will know that you are my disciples, if you have love for one another.
John 13:35

We've all heard the statement, "Actions speak louder than words." Love is a great example. Too many times, love is used as a noun and not a verb. Love is both. Our actions demonstrate the true conviction of our heart, both in our relationship with God and with others. Our words are powerful. And how much more powerful can they be if they are backed up by actions? We are called to be God's messengers and encouragers. Maybe not all at once, but certainly when the need arises, we are to share His love and encouragement. It's a beautiful way of living out the command to love one another. When we go through struggles, we all need someone to come alongside to remind us there is hope ahead. Painful lessons are usually doorways to new opportunities.

Testimony

And so you will bear testimony to me.
Luke 21:13 (NIV)

While Trey was home for college fall break, one of his friends told me of the struggles he went through at a very difficult school. It broke my heart to hear of this since I care about this young man. We talked about why this had happened. I believe when God allows us to go through problems, struggles, and difficulties, we learn to depend on Him. We learn our own limits and are reminded to look to Him for what we need most. He uses our wounds to make us stronger and to help those around us. This same young man acknowledged to us the importance of encouragement and how he is determined to reach out to others who are struggling and make a difference. Our greatest pleasure in life comes from serving others, giving them what no one else can provide in that exact time and place. His test has certainly become his testimony.

This week I encourage you to share one of your struggles with someone as a means of encouraging or motivating that person. You never know the difference a kind word, listening ear, or a shoulder to lean on can make.

Testimony

I am the one who bears witness about myself, and the Father who sent me bears witness about me.
John 8:18

How can you use your past experiences to help others? I love it in church when people share their testimonies and are willing to display how the Lord has worked wonders in their life. I have been thinking about my own life testimony and realize some people think their testimony is just a brief account of the way God has worked in their life. While that is true, our testimony is much more than simply a short story. Our character is one aspect of our testimony. Do we follow God's instruction and His guidance, no matter what? Our daily conduct is another facet of our testimony. If what we say conflicts with our behavior, we cloud our witness and are hypocritical. The way we act should confirm who we are in Christ. Our testimony can make the difference between doubt and faith in the lives of others. What is your personal testimony? Are you willing to share it to help others?

Your test becomes your testimony.

Loyalty

Whoever pursues righteousness and kindness will find life, righteousness, and honor.
Proverbs 21:21

Genuine loyalty is not built around circumstances, popularity, or convenience. True loyalty is built on devotion to God and love and respect for others.

Over the last twenty years I've had the privilege of being a part of a small Bible study group with amazing, loyal, God-centered women that I love. Through the years we have celebrated life's victories, provided shelter during life's storms, prayed and supported one another, encouraged one another, and allowed ourselves to be vulnerable and transparent. I treasure these relationships. Their loyalty over the years has never wavered. It's been beautiful to witness the steady involvement and commitment to our relationships with Christ and each other. We are active participants in a like-minded community dedicated to spiritual growth. Application and accountability bring understanding that moves God's Word from the intellect to the heart.

Relationships don't just happen; they require time, trust, and loyalty. Loyalty is not a word, it's a lifestyle.

Loyalty

Be strong and courageous. Do not fear or be in dread of them, for it is the LORD your God who goes with you. He will not leave or forsake you.
Deuteronomy 31:6

Loyalty is a precious commodity—a trait worth reflecting on in our own lives and beautiful to witness in others. Many profess it, but few have it. I read about a dog that accidentally wandered onto the freeway in LA; tragically, he was hit and killed. His companion dog ran out in the middle of traffic and sat by his side. She would not leave his side. Animal control came and picked up both dogs. They named the surviving dog Grace, as she proved her loyalty to her friend even at the risk of getting run over herself.

Being devoted to something means we are loyal to it by the giving of our time, affection, and resources. Let's examine our hearts today and see if we are being devoted to what God has called us to. Are we devoted to the people God has placed in our life? Do we honor others above ourselves? As we choose to live a life devoted to one another, we are honoring God.

Impact

As each has received a gift, use it to serve one another, as good stewards of God's varied grace.
1 Peter 4:10

The Tim Tebow Foundation celebrates its annual Night to Shine, a prom centered on God's love for those with special needs. More than one hundred thousand guests from all over the world get to walk down a red carpet and be crowned as kings and queens. Every year I look forward to volunteering. It's quite a different form of red carpet, where we usually see movie stars seeking to make an impression. To seek to make an impression is to make a display. To seek to make an impact—to affect someone positively—is to make a difference. Making an impression is what we do for ourselves. Making an impact is what we do for others. To seek to make an impact centers on Christ. Impressions don't change lives, positive impacts do.

Think about what and who has affected your life and whose life you are affecting. As we abide in Jesus, He shines through to positively affect those around us.

Impact

The name of the LORD is a strong tower; the righteous man runs into it and is safe.
Proverbs 18:10

JT Townsend influenced many lives, especially mine. I learned so much from him over the years: about honoring and trusting God, about faith, about love, about kindness, about honesty, perseverance, forgiveness, and loyalty. He acknowledged God as all knowing, all present, all faithful, all loving, regardless of his circumstance. He lived by the Scripture: I can do all things through Christ Who gives me strength. I remember dancing with him as he swirled around me, laughing, in his wheelchair. He ran his race with a pure heart and clean hands. He lived a life of true character, he honored God, and he stole my heart. Jacksonville's mayor honored his birthday as "JT Townsend Day."

JT was an amazing young man and a true ambassador for Christ.

Inspiration

And let us consider how to stir up one another to love and good works.
Hebrews 10:24

As I walked into a hotel lobby, these words were lit up on the floor: "What inspires you?" Immediately after reading this, I went outside and met a man who had his Bible opened and notes scattered on the table. He was deep in the Word. After a nice chat with Dr. A. B. Sutton Jr., the pastor of Living Stones Temple, I left inspired.

When you inspire someone, you leave a positive impression on their mind and their soul. Being inspired transcends your net worth, job title, marital status, or outward appearance. An inspired person can be dropped anywhere, at any time, in any circumstance, and still be inspiring because they are inspired on the inside. Their inspiration is not an outward veneer that can be stolen or a fragile emotion that adversity can sweep away. A truly inspired person is someone who has life breathed into them on the inside.

God's inspiration is always others centered. He seeks to implant seeds of inspiration to change the lives of others. To inspire is to be a magnet that draws others closer to Christ.

This week, think about what inspires you and, better yet, who do you inspire?

Inspiration

I praise you, for I am fearfully and wonderfully made.
Wonderful are your works; my soul knows it very well.
Psalm 139:14

McKenzie Noelle Wilson, in her short life, inspired everyone she touched with her beautiful spirit, love for Christ, and unconditional love. Something truly remarkable about McKenzie was the way she chose to live her life. Although McKenzie was called home to the Lord at the age of 15, she affected more lives than others do in a lifetime—through her random acts of kindness, charity, and love toward those in need. The inspiration behind the foundation created in her name was the theme "Care, Give, Grow." She wrote in her Bible that she wanted to make her faith public; that's exactly what she did, and her legacy lives on.

Jesus tells us to love one another just as He loves us. How does He love us? Unconditionally. Do we love like that? Or do we expect people to earn our love? How do we show unconditional love and kindness? By loving people even when they don't deserve it. By being willing to forgive. By caring for the poor, the elderly, the misfits, and others, with no thought of material reward. We can perform acts of kindness that are difficult, tedious, unglamorous, and inconvenient; we can honor one another, encourage one another, and freely forgive one another.

When we love others this way, they see Christ in us. I thank God for His unconditional love, and remember the many other beautiful life lessons I learned from McKenzie.

Thank you for joining me on this journey. I hope you've been inspired by the many blessings along the way, and enjoyed the ride!

Made in the USA
Columbia, SC
05 February 2023

11815999R00067